Happiness is Free

Happiness is Free

21 Principles to Experience It the Easy Way

PROVIN KAMI

PARTRIDGE

A Penguin Random House Company

ISBN: Softcover   978-1-4828-4529-7
               eBook   978-1-4828-4528-0

Print information available on the last page.

To order additional copies of this book, contact
Partridge India
000 800 10062 62
orders.india@partridgepublishing.com

www.partridgepublishing.com/india

CONTENTS

To my parents

ACKNOWLEDGEMENTS

I am blessed to have a happy attitude. The major credit goes to my parents for giving me wonderful upbringing and umpteen happy moments.

I am grateful to my elder brother, Shri Rovin Kami, a true friend, philosopher and guide, whose ability to hustle and hard work has always inspired me.

This book would not have seen the light of the day without the support of my wife Sanjukta, who sacrificed our weekend outings & pushed me to conclude my eternal-book-writing mission.

I am grateful to my sister-in-law Smt. Rekha Kami, nephew Hrudityaa and Sister, Reena Kami for bringing so much happiness to our family.

I am grateful to all my school friends (especially Narayan Dana and Satinder Pal Singh and 1995-97 batch mates) for co-creating such a joyful time at Kendriya Vidhyalaya, Mount Abu and batch mates (1997-2000) from Cotton College, Guwahati.

My tribute to my Late friend Rakesh, the happy guy who succumb to unhappy circumstances.

I thank my friends from Mumbai Toastmasters club.

I am grateful to my friends from 2005 batch and all the officers and staff members of DBS, Chennai, RBI (2007-2011) and DBR, CO, RBI, Mumbai for making me wiser and happier.

Provin Kami

Finally, Shri F.R Joseph, Ex- PCGM, RBI and Shri Vivek Aggarwal, GM, RBI deserves special mention and gratitude. I have learnt so much from their positive attitude and excellent people-skill.

THE PROMISE

Happiness is free, and it is easy.

The promise statement might seem like a Ponzi scheme's claim of 25 per cent return per annum. Furthermore, the higher your intelligence, the greater the unwillingness to buy this promise. Anyway, too much intellect has always been a rival of feelings, including happiness.

The main inspiration behind writing this book is the paradox of happiness, which often perplexes me that how come sages at Himalaya live a very vibrant and blissful life without any bank balance, insurance, and no guarantee of a next meal? How come Mother Teresa left her cushy job and the ambience of missionary life and got involved in pulling dead bodies out of the gutter and giving them dignified cremation, feeding leprosy patients, and led a very happy life whereas the world winners like Elvis Presley, Marilyn Monroe, and Michael Jackson had very miserable personal lives? Yeah, you might call it biased sampling of a few people. But look around, and you will realize many such paradoxical examples around you. Simplify your life and reassess at what it really costs to be happy.

Is happiness directly connected to material prosperity? Is our attitude and belief system more important when it comes to happiness? Can there be a simple solution to the complex topic of being happy?

Here's an interesting story (though there are various versions) of the Astronaut pen, which emphasize on common sense and wisdom to tackle problems with simple solutions:

During the space rivalry back in the 1960s, when NASA started sending astronauts into space, they faced with a challenge of inventing a ball-point pens which would work in zero Gravity in space. It is said that NASA scientists spent millions in developing an Astronaut pen that writes in zero gravity, upside down, and on almost any surface, including glass, and at temperatures ranging from below freezing to over 300°C.

The Russians solved the same problem by using a pencil.

So the question is, do we need to go through all the pain and the long path of a so-called success journey to feel the most fundamental feeling called happiness? Remember, humans are the only species in the universe who can smile.

But we tend to make it so unreachable and complicated by buying the social definition of happiness. We attach our happiness to the moving milestone and feel empty when all energy and enthusiasm is spent in the process of attaining the successive goals. Happiness is a natural, free, and simple thing to attain. It depends on you and the path you take—the pen path or the pencil one. You have to choose between out-there happiness, tagged with achievement milestones or right-here happiness, string with the present moment.

Intellectually, let me tell that a little effort in the right direction can significantly bolster your happiness level. The trick is to use the Pareto Law, popularly called the 80–20 principle. It states that 80 per cent of efforts results in 20 per cent of results. Similarly, it can be said that 80 per cent of misery is caused by 20 per cent of action/causes. Mathematically, even if you reduce these actions/causes from 20 per cent to 10 per cent, it can reduce your unhappiness by 30 to 40 per cent and add to the kitty of happiness.

Similarly, 20 per cent of efforts lead to 80 per cent of happiness. Hence, focusing on critical factors of happiness is pivotal for achieving it faster and retaining it. The methods suggested in this book are extremely simple, and they are free. At the end of the book, you may evaluate whether the promise is true or not.

The book is about embracing twenty-one principles of happiness, which covers your physical, mental, social, and spiritual dimensions. It enhances your understanding about the concept of happiness—how association with people, thoughts and attitude towards self, others, and changing circumstances; body; posture; and work can go a long way to ensure happiness without accumulating millions and spending them on luxuries. Go through these principles, and most importantly, practice them consistently. You will realize that happiness was never so hard to attain as it might have seemed. It is more like cleaning the dust from the lens to view and experience happiness around us. Most importantly, be comfortable while applying these principles. Don't try too hard, as the middle path is the way to happy life. 'To go beyond is as wrong as to fall short' (Confucius).

INTRODUCTION

Happiness

The only duty you have is to be happy. Make it a religion to be happy. If you are not happy, whatsoever you are doing, something must be wrong and some drastic change is needed. Let happiness decide.

So always look at what happens when you do something: if you become peaceful or restful at home, relaxed, it is right. This is the criterion; nothing else is the criterion (Osho).

Happiness is the courageous decision that

If I feel depressed, I will sing.
If I feel sad, I will laugh.
If I feel ill, I will double my labour.
If I feel fear, I will plunge ahead.
If I feel inferior, I will wear new garments.
If I feel uncertain, I will raise my voice.
If I feel poverty, I will think of wealth to come.
If I feel incompetent, I will remember my past success.
If I feel insignificant, I will remember my goals.
Today I will be the master of emotions.

(Og Mandino, *The Greatest Salesman in the World*)

Movement from Development to Well-Being

The development economics has moved from Gross National Product (GNP) to Human Development Index to Gross National Happiness (GNH). The World Happiness Report 2013 states the following:

> In July 2011 the UN General Assembly passed a historic resolution. It invited member countries to measure the happiness of their people and to use this to help guide their public policies. This was followed in April 2012 by the first UN high-level meeting on happiness and well-being, chaired by the Prime Minister of Bhutan. At the same time the first World Happiness Report was published, followed some months later by the OECD Guidelines setting an international standard for the measurement of well-being.

The World Happiness Report 2013 further emphasizes that 'happiness is an aspiration of every human being, and can also be a measure of social progress'. The paradox of prosperity coexisting with depression is also highlighted in the report as it says, 'America's founding fathers declared the inalienable right to pursue happiness. Yet are Americans, or citizens of other countries, happy? If they are not, what if anything can be done about it?'

The OECD Guidelines

The World Happiness Report 2013 states that the OECD approach to measuring subjective well-being covers a wider range of concepts than just happiness. In particular, the focus is on subjective well-being, which is taken to be

> good mental states, including all of the various evaluations, positive and negative, that people make of their lives and the affective reactions of people to their experiences.

This definition is intended to be inclusive, encompassing the full range of different aspects of subjective well-being commonly identified by research in this field. It includes, first and foremost, measures of how people experience and evaluate their life as a whole. However, the scope of the definition also covers measures of meaningfulness or purpose in life (often described as eudaemonic aspects of subjective well-being).

This definition of subjective well-being hence encompasses three elements:

- *Life evaluation*—a reflective assessment on a person's life or some specific aspect of it
- *Affect*—a person's feelings or emotional states, typically measured with reference to a particular point in time
- *Eudaemonia*—a sense of meaning and purpose in life, or good psychological functioning

Fulfilled

The feeling of fullness creates happiness. The sense of completeness gives confidence and certainty leading to happiness. The feeling of being fulfilled(ness) is an attitude and disposition. The principles of happiness go through the various elements of happiness. If you follow these principles, you can attain lasting happiness in your life. 'You have to learn the rules of the game. And then you have to play better than anyone else' (Albert Einstein).

The positive impact of happiness is now being documented by the new genre of happiness researchers. It is observed that happy people live longer; they are the cynosure; they are more productive, they create positive environment around and more successful in professional and personal life. The book by Shawn Achor, *The Happiness Advantage: The Seven Principles of Positive Psychology*, challenges the universal assumption that success automatically leads to happiness. We know from the experience that success ≠ happiness—rather happiness generates lasting success. Happiness is not just the destination of success but the means of attaining success as well. 'Success is not the key to happiness. Happiness is the key to success. If you love what you are doing, you will be successful' (Albert Schweitzer). Don't put the key to your happiness in someone else's hand.

The credo of 'success first, happiness later' fails to ensure fulfilling life. We have seen that most of the icons of success and fame lead a very miserable private life. This phenomenon is ubiquitous among the youth born with silver spoons. The most prosperous countries like the USA are struggling with drug addiction, gun culture, divorce, suicide, etc. The path of successful public life does not guarantee happiness rather it increases the chances of severe backlash in case of decline in fame and wealth or failure in relationships. Giving more importance to your private life rather than public life seems more logical for lasting happiness and success. Grow happiness in your feet rather than placing it on the outer world.

The renowned French naturalist, Jean-Henri Fabre, once conducted a groundbreaking experiment. He used processionary caterpillars to move through the forest in a long procession feeding on pine needles. Processionary caterpillars. They derive their name from their habit of following a lead caterpillar, each with its head fitted against the rear end of the preceding caterpillar. They move with the same pace, giving no attention to the final destination. Jean-Henri Fabre took a giant flower pot and placed substantial amount of food in the centre of the pot. He took the lead caterpillar to connect up with the last one, creating a complete circle, which moved around the pot in a never-ending procession. He thought that after a few circles of the pot, the caterpillars would tire of their endless progression and move off in another direction. But they never deviated from their path and continued with their movement. Even after seven days, they were moving on the rim of the pot and did not break the pattern to eat food that lay in the centre of the pot. Finally in the end, they died of starvation and exhaustion. Like the processionary caterpillars, we too run after the circular path of shifting goal of success even though the food of soul, the happiness lies near to us in the centre. We tirelessly keep on moving on and on, never looking inward, at the centre. 'The foolish man seeks happiness in the distance, the wise man grows it under his feet' (James Oppenheim).

The phenomenon of ever striving and never arriving is sapping and creates oasis illusion. It is shown by following the simple illustration.

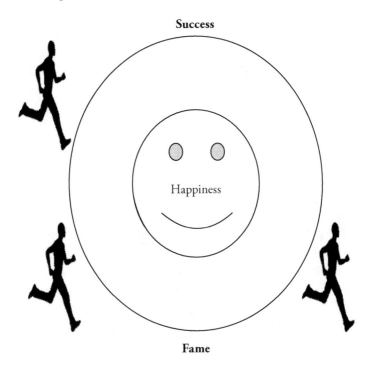

The happiness route ensures that you enjoy each moment. It is arriving each moment and then striving with full energy. 'Life is a journey, not a destination' (Ralph Waldo Emerson).

The concept of success needs to be changed. We need to define it as per our deepest craving and strength zone. The problems arise when we run after the success admired by the society rather than success or the destination our soul would feel happy about.

Effects of Well-Being

Chapter 4 of *The World Happiness Report 2013* considers the objective benefits of subjective well-being. The chapter presents a broad range of evidence showing that the people who are emotionally happier, who have more satisfying lives, and who live in happier communities are more likely, both now and later, to be healthy, productive, and socially connected. These benefits, in turn, flow more broadly to their families, workplaces, and communities to the advantage of all.

The very concept of success needs to be defined in terms of totality of life rather than just monetary terms or fame.

What is success?

To laugh often and much; to win the respect of intelligent people and the affection of children; to earn the appreciation of honest critics and endure the betrayal of false friends; to appreciate the beauty; to find the best in others; to leave the world a bit better, whether by a healthy child, a garden patch. Or a redeemed social condition; to know even one life has breathed easier because you have lived. This is to have succeeded! (Ralph Waldo Emerson)

Every action has its intrinsic reward or punishment. So a man of intelligence soon starts finding what are the acts that bring you happiness, joy, and bliss and what are the actions that create misery and suffering. There is no need to wait for the last judgment day, there is no need to wait after death—you will be thrown into hell or into heaven. 'Each moment completes itself' (Osho).

The goal of this book is to attain lasting happiness. The book suggests a two-pronged approach. First, enhancing the source of happiness, and second, curtailing the source of unhappiness. Happiness does not mean the total absence of challenges. Just like an arrow has to be pulled back to go forward, sadness and struggles increase the depth of our experience of happiness.

PART I

Understanding Happiness

PRINCIPLE 1

Understanding the Paradox

Here's the catch! All the treasure is within us; still, we hanker for the treasure outside. It is so easy but still not so obvious for mankind. God has tweaked it a little for fun or letting the world go around a bit. He wants us to run after it a little, exert, and then look inward for the treasure. Just like the deer that has fragrance in its navel but runs hither to thither thinking that the fragrance lies out there, we too think in the same way. Happiness is out there. The material possessions are there to enhance our experience of happiness. The wealth undoubtedly prevents us from unnecessary pain and daily struggles. It provides a foundation for enjoying a good life but does not guarantee it. Attaching happiness to possession of things brings only misery and leads to running after a mirage. The more you possess or try to possess, the more you feel empty. 'Real freedom is having nothing. I was freer when I didn't have a cent' (Mike Tyson). It is just like bartering a map for the territory. The mad rush for the material possession is an act of covering the inner emptiness. It slowly becomes cyclic and self-reinforcing. In this hunt for possession of things, your being is lost.

Here's an interesting story about acquisition of wealth, power, and territory, which does not guarantee happiness:

Alexander was a great and ambitious king and best known for his military expedition for conquering the world. He conquered many countries. However, due to his illness he had to pause. Soon he realized that he might succumb to his illness. He decided to return home to see his mother before breathing his last. But when he saw the death may knock at him anytime and may not be able to return to his homeland, he felt that his vast captured territories and wealth all had little meaning. He told his officers the he had three final wishes:

1. Let my physician bring my coffin home alone.
2. Scatter the gold, silver, and gems along the path to the tomb.
3. Put my hands outside the coffin.

His generals were perplexed at these wishes and requested their king the reason behind these wishes. Alexander explained them the he wanted people to understand the three lessons he has learned. The first wish was to let people realize that a physician cannot really save people from death. The message is that we should live our life fully. The second wish was to demonstrate to people that a life engaged in only chasing wealth robs you of your important moments of your life. The message is that wealth should not be the only goal of life and we need to cherish the beauty of life as well. The third wish was to show people that Alexander the Great came to this world with empty hands and despite conquering the vast territories would leave this world empty-handed. The message is you cannot take anything with you, so strive for a fulfilling life. Place happiness before material possessions because the goal of life is happiness and not success. All the success and material comfort is for deriving more happiness. Therefore, approach directly the goal of happiness rather than getting stuck in the means.

Here's another interesting story:

An American investment banker was sitting near beach in a coastal Mexican village. He saw one fisherman returning to the shore in his small boat. The American complimented the fisherman on his fish and asked how long it took to catch them.

The fisherman replied, "Little time." The American surprisingly asked why didn't he stay out longer to catch more fish? The fisherman said he had enough to support his family's immediate needs. The American then asked, "but what do you do with spare time?"

The fisherman said, "I sleep late, fish a little, play with my children, stroll into the village, enjoy wine, and play guitar." The American mockingly said, "I am an investment banker and could help you. You should spend more time fishing and with the earned money you would buy a bigger boat and then buy more boats. Subsequently, you would sell fish directly to the processor. Hence, you would be able to control the product, processing, and distribution and move to the city and run your company."

The fisherman asked, "But, how much time will this all take?"

American replied, "15 – 20 years."

The fisherman said, "But what then?".

The American laughed and said, "You would then announce an IPO and sell your company stock to the public and become millionaire."

"Millionaire – then what?"

The American said, "Then you would retire and move to a small coastal fishing village where you would sleep late, fish a little, play with your kids, stroll to the village in the evenings, enjoy wine and play your guitar."

Hence, happiness can be approached directly rather than treading the beaten path everybody follows. Enjoy each moment with whatever you have and whatever you are.

'When your needs are less, you are able to take bigger responsibilities' (Sri Sri Ravi Shankar). Too much focus on success and money is a sign of an inner lack, which we tend to compensate for by acquiring more name and fame. When our private life is not very satisfactory or happy, we tend to get obsessed with our public life.

One of the biggest myths is more money betters personality and creates happiness. Money is not a transformer; rather, it is a multiplier. It gives you avenue and space to multiply or expand your very self. Money does not guarantee inner growth but expansion of what you already are. 'The problem with winning the rat race is you're still a rat' (Lily Tomlin).

'Of the billionaires I have known, money just brings out the basic traits in them. If they were jerks before they had money, they are simply jerks with a billion dollars' (Warren Buffett).

Humans tend to think we are the masters of the universe when they cannot even master themselves. We all tempt to go for the ego trip of conquering the external world like the king Alexander but fail to realize that the treasure of happiness is inside us.

There are two things that need to be understood: (1) running after pleasure reduces happiness, and (2) being minimalist and simple augments happiness.

1. *Pleasure is the enemy of happiness.* The sadder you are, the more you will hanker for the pleasure. The cheap and quick pleasure of watching excessive television or movies, drugs, sex, theft, and killing and dominating others through violence are all the signs of pleasure. 'Pleasure is the happiness of madmen, while happiness is the pleasure of sages' (Jules-Amédée Barbey d'Aurevilly). The gun culture of American school is the symbol of frustration among boys or the American youth to steal the limelight and to get importance. The problem is that over a period it becomes self-propagating. The more you indulge into pleasurable activities, the more frustrated you become and look further for more escapism through pleasure.

'The superior man cannot be known in little matters, but he may be entrusted with great concerns. The small man may not be entrusted with great concerns, but he may be known in little matters' (Confucius).

2. *Being minimalist and simple.* The concept of linear programming illustrates a vital learning point. It is the mathematical technique used in computer modelling (simulation) to find the best possible solution in allocating

limited resources (energy, machines, materials, money, personnel, space, time, etc.) to achieve maximum profit or minimum cost. It achieves the goal within the given constraints. In life too these constraints or limitations bring out the best in us. As Anthony Robbins says, it is not the resources but resourcefulness that is more important. 'I believe that a simple and unassuming life is good for everybody, physically and mentally' (Albert Einstein).

The paradox of happiness and material possession is ubiquitous. We buy more things but enjoy less. We have varieties of food but less appetite. We have more gadgets for connecting and communicating but we relate less with each other. It is common to see that family members and friends dinning together but remain obsessed with their smartphone. We have more education but display less common sense. Style is valued more than the substance. We have more comfort but fragile health. Our economic conditions have drastically improved but we are grappled with poor relationships. Simple life is way to a happy life.

Because 'Not what we have but what we enjoy, constitutes our abundance' (Epicurus).

PRINCIPLE 2

Happiness Is Intangible and It's Free

'The best and most beautiful things in the world cannot be seen or even touched. They must be felt with the heart' (Helen Keller).

How much money does it take to enjoy the beauty of nature? It can be a rose in your balcony or a mountain at a distance or little puppies in the backyard? How much money does it cost to smile at the fellow passenger, neighbour, or patient next to your bed? How much money does it take to help an elderly person to cross the road and feel the satisfaction of having helped?

The locus of happiness is inside, and all you have to do is to shift the focus. Happiness is the way of life, and we can experience it any time at our will. You need to shift your focus to the present. If I say shift the focus away from negativity or unhappiness because it is not good for you, the majority would not listen. However, if I say that it is utter stupidity, then your ego may be more willing to listen. It is indeed stupid because you are carrying the garbage of others as a precious diamond. A person who might have hurt you in the past, but that moment has passed and holds no relevance except for the learning. It is you who has chosen to hold on to that moment and suffer. For example, if in your childhood your friend has hurt you and now you relive it, is it rational on your part? Life is a continuous flow. You have to focus on the present, and if you remain in the past, you will miss the beautiful present. Make your happiness unconditional. The materialistic society has made the happiness a rare commodity. Happiness has been defined in parameters of social status, political clout, and wealth. As a result, we are in the eternal rat race. We have attached our happiness to achievement and not experience. We have restricted or limited our feeling of happiness on future milestones, which itself keeps on moving to the next. Thus, we remain starved in experiencing happiness and chase the oasis. The best approach to life is to enjoy, no matter what happens within you or around you. Learn from nature. Observe a flower—whether you are rich or poor, famous or unknown, powerful or weak, it does not give its fragrance selectively. It is non-discriminatory because it is just as it is. It just gives without any thought of return. 'When love is my only defence, I am invincible' (Tao).

Immunize your happiness with the circumstances and events. Make your happiness unconditional; otherwise you will be moving with the waves of external circumstance. 'Wise men put their trust in ideas and not in circumstances' (Ralph Waldo Emerson).

Happiness is free and intangible, and it can be attained and retained with a simple routine and mindset. Daily exercise, meditation, patience, usage of good words, and positive self-talk does not cost you a single penny but tremendously enhances your happiness.

PRINCIPLE 3

Happiness Is an Attitude

'The mind is its own place, and in itself can make a heaven of hell, a hell of heaven' (John Milton). The most important trait for happiness in life is that of a positive attitude because it is not what the reality is but what we think or perceive about the event in life. Our reaction is dependent upon our attitude and not necessarily on the actual event. Happiness is, therefore, dependent on attitude, and attitude is built up on our habit. Positive habits lead to positive attitude, which makes happiness easy. Life is an attitude. Hence, a happy attitude begets a happy life. 'People are just as happy as they make up their minds to be' (Abraham Lincoln). The happiest of people don't necessarily have the best of everything; they just make the most of everything that comes along their way. Happiness is a way of life. Happiness is your responsibility. Nobody would offer happiness to you. As Og Mandino rightly said, 'Trees and plants depend on the weather to flourish but I make my own weather, yea I transport it with me.'

Sean Covey, in his book *The Seven Habits of Effective Teens*, has defined *habit* below:

Who Am I?

I am your constant companion. I am your greatest helper or heaviest burden. I will push you forward or drag you down to failure. I am completely at your command. Half the things you do, you might just as well turn over to me and I will be able to do them quickly and correctly.

I am easily managed—you must merely be firm with me. Show me exactly how you want something done and after a few lessons I will do it automatically. I am the servant of all great individuals, and alas, of all failures as well. Those who are great, I have made great. Those who are failures, I have made failures.

I am not a machine, though I work with all the precision of a machine plus the intelligence of a human. You may run me for profit or run me for ruin—it makes no difference to me.

Take me, train me, be firm with me, and I will place the world at your feet. Be easy with me and I will destroy you.

Who am I?
I am habit.

If you develop positive thinking, you will end up with a positive attitude, which would enable you to overcome any obstacle and look at the positive aspect of life and events.

'If you are unhappy, that simply means that you have learned tricks for being unhappy. Nothing else! Unhappiness depends on the frame of your mind. There are people who are unhappy in all kinds of situations. They have a certain program in their mind that transforms everything into unhappiness. If you tell them about the beauty of the rose, they immediately start counting the thorns . . . All depends on what kind of frame you are carrying in your head' (Osho).

The happy attitude entails two major action points or traits:

1. *The wisdom of changing the story*. Emotional intelligence enables us to minimize the emotional suffering because control is in our hands, and to what extent events would make an impact depends on our interpretation. The moment you change perspective toward an event—from a problem to a challenge—your emotions undergo transformation from being miserable and helpless to being confident and resourceful. In human relationships, we are primarily driven to think of our interests, and we have our viewpoints and the way things should happen, the way people should behave, the way climate should be when you are on vacation. This 'should be' is a very egoistic and unbalanced way of living in the world. It is a sure shot for being miserable. Recognize that you are not the creator of this universe. How nature and events unfold, how people should behave is too much for us to bother with. The entire edifice of Neuro Linguistic Programming (NLP) is on the fact that most of our life is

nothing but interpretation of what is happening to us and around us. If we could recognize this fact and exercise the ability to change the interpretation and perception of what is happening in our mind, then our life would be much more fulfilling and successful.

Positive attitude would enable you to accept different things, people, or events. An open mind is a prerequisite to enjoy happiness. The nature's way is that of acceptance. 'What matters in life is not what happens to you but what you remember and how you remember it' (Gabriel Garcia Marquez). The perception of what is happening is more important than what is happening. The feel-good factor leading to real improvement in health is well-documented and known as the placebo effect. It is not the reality but your notion that impacts us. For instance, if you take a rope for a snake in a dark room, you will try to escape from the snake and experience tremendous fear. If you think they are real, they function for you as reality. Hence, your belief or notion impacts you as reality.

'For him who has conquered the mind, the mind is the best of friends; but for one who has failed to do so, his mind will remain the greatest enemy' (Bhagavad Gita)

You've got to realize that you must take conscious control of running your own mind. You've got to do it deliberately; otherwise, you're going to be at the mercy of whatever happens around you. The NLP says that we can change our mental state instantly, provided we are convinced and practice controlling our reaction to the event. We must apply some mental trick to shift our focus to good memories like touching our lucky bracelet, wearing our favourite shirt, kissing the cross, praying to God, or talking to our mentor or parents to significantly improve our mental state.

TRUTH in her dress finds facts too tight.
In fiction she moves with ease.

(Rabindranath Tagore)

Reality bites; never strive to live in the naked truth. Ideal situation and people just do not exist. As J. Krishnamurty aptly said, 'There is no experience if there is no recognition. If I do not recognize, I have no experience. Have I? You only say "I have an experience" when there is a process of recognition taking place. Our difficulty is to understand desire without this process of recognition.'

Nothing in life has a meaning except for the meaning we give or attached to it. For a child, the earthen elephant is like a real elephant. When it breaks, he cries as if it had life. That is his reality because of the meaning he attached to it. When I was a child, I remember how I used to cry when an actor died on the screen. I particularly remember a movie where the actor beat his dog and then the dog died saving his life. I took those scenes as real, and I felt pain and cried. However, today my notion and understanding have changed, and I would not cry about such a movie scene.

2. *Positive belief code.* Life is ruled by your beliefs. They set the templates of your life. Beliefs are tremendously powerful. As he rightly said, 'One person with a belief is equal to ninety-nine who have only interests.' Belief has two segments: belief about yourself and belief about the world.

What do you think about yourself?
Do you love yourself?
Do you respect yourself?
Do you consider yourself as successful?

These are the essential questions that are deeply connected with your self-image. All perceptions about happiness relate to our sense of self-worth. A positive self-image is essential to happiness and should be cultivated. It can be done—give up all your guilt and focus on your strengths.

The second aspect is what your beliefs about the world are. The inherent belief system has a huge impact on our entire personality, behaviour, and disposition of life. What do you truly believe? If you believe that the world around is against you, then you will be fearful, doubting, and stressful. Whereas if you truly believe that world is essentially good, then you will be trusting, open, and confident. In Sanskrit, *fear* means 'two'. How does fear come? The fear comes out of a feeling of separateness. If you have deep conviction, you are separate from the universe, and it works against you. Then you will experience havoc because you won't trust others and you will be fearful and doubtful towards them. But if you develop a belief that you are one with the universe and there is no other, you will feel peaceful and secure.

'The single most important decision any of us will ever to make is whether or not to believe that the universe is friendly' (Albert Einstein).

PRINCIPLE 4

Being Creative and Courageous

'When life gives you a hundred reasons to cry, show life that you have a thousand reasons to smile' (Stephenie Meyer). When I got transferred to Mumbai in the year 2011, I was anxious about travelling in crowded Mumbai trains as suggested by my office colleagues. The first two days I was very confused about the foot bridges and the exit. I was so tired that I forgot to take dinner and slept like a horse even though my train journey was of a shorter distance of fourteen kilometres vis-à-vis the usual long-distance travel of thirty to sixty kilometres in Mumbai. But soon I realized that even this journey could be used creatively. Often when I used to board the long-distance fast train, I saw a variety of ways people would creatively transform this suffocating journey into an enjoyable one. I saw that many people sleep to restore energy, a few read newspaper or books for their exams, traders execute orders through their mobiles, and a few groups sing spiritual songs, and the journey, instead of becoming boring and painful, becomes memorable and elating. There are many instances wherein the retired people travel in their group to enjoy the playing cards and sing songs and gossip. They build lifetime relationships and make this ordeal of a journey the most memorable moment of their everyday life. Chuck Palahniuk once said, 'The only way to find true happiness in life is to risk being completely cut open.' Pain and challenges are not unhappiness; it is the attitude and wisdom we apply to those uncomfortable situations. 'If you hear a voice within you say "You cannot paint," then by all means paint and that voice will be silenced' (Vincent Van Gogh).

'Whatever you do, you need courage. Whatever course you decide upon, there is always someone to tell you that you are wrong. There are always difficulties arising that tempt you to believe your critics are right. To map out a course of action and follow it to an end requires some of the same courage that a soldier needs. Peace has its victories, but it takes brave men and women to win them' (Ralph Waldo Emerson).

You must decide for yourself whether your behaviour is right or wrong, whether it is effective or ineffective in the pursuit of legitimate goals. Enjoy yourself whatever be the circumstances. When you are creative, you can bring out the best out of every situation. Furthermore, the courage will give confidence to face any circumstances and come out victorious. 'Out of your vulnerabilities will come your strength' (Sigmund Freud). The creative and courageous person would ask, 'How can I make this into a great experience?' rather than shrinking into their comfort zone. 'To choose doubt as a philosophy of life is akin to choosing immobility as a means of transportation' (Yann Martel).

'People are always blaming their circumstances for what they are. I don't believe in circumstances. The people who get on in this world are the people who get up and look for the circumstances they want, and if they can't find them, make them' (George Bernard Shaw).

We need to also know that discomforts and challenges are bound to be part of our life. That cannot be called as unhappiness; if we are patient, creative, and courageous, the valleys of suffering would make the peaks of happiness more meaningful. Be a warrior, and be ready for absolute vulnerability.

Life is not a bed of roses; it is full of challenges. Happiness is not for the chicken-hearted, it is for the eagles, which fly when the storm begins. The strong winds drive away all the other birds; the king of birds takes on the challenge, and fast winds further support the eagle's wings to fly above the storm. The eagle derives strength from the storm. The nature and the world move around the strong because strength is life. The fundamental truth of life and the law of attraction is best described in these words: 'Whoever has will be given more; whoever does not have, even what they have will be taken from them' (Holy Bible).

'I am determined to be cheerful and happy in whatever situation I may find myself. For I have learned that the greater part of our misery or unhappiness is determined not by our circumstance but by our disposition' (Martha Washington).

Hence, be creative and courageous and transform every challenge and obstacle into an opportunity and memorable event. The choice and power are within; all you need is wisdom and boldness. 'A coward dies a thousand times before his death, but the valiant taste of death but once. It seems to me most strange that men should fear, seeing that death, a necessary end, will come when it will come' (William Shakespeare).

PRINCIPLE 5

Happiness By-product— Indirect Happiness

Happiness is like attracting women. If you are too upfront and needy, you lose the game. Likewise, happiness is a by-product of right living and thoughts and action. 'Happiness is like a butterfly; the more you chase it, the more it will elude you, but if you turn your attention to other things, it will come and sit softly on your shoulder' (H. D. Thoreau).

The eightfold path of Buddhism is the cornerstone of perennial happiness.

1. *Right view*. It is the right perspective or the right way of looking at life, nature, and the world as they really are. It is to understand reality and practise to accept it and go beyond it. It is understanding that suffering, sickness, aging, and death are part of our life and humans are driven by greed, hatred, fear, and delusion.

2. *Right intention*. Right intention is right resolve or aspiration. It is our own will to change for the better and

towards goodness. Right intention is purity of thought and aspiring to become free from negative thoughts and intention. Wrong intention is the path to unhappiness. Right intention towards self and others is the way to harmony and happiness.

3. *Right speech.* Right speech deals with the way in which a person would best make use of their words. The words are the crown of our personality. The ways you speak determine your relationship, sales, and progress in life. When we use wrong and abusive language, it leads to argument and fights. Telling lies is another way to bringing negative influence in our life. The right speech comes with silence and moderation in speech. The importance of words is further explained in detail under the principle 19.

4. *Right action.* Right action is basically right conduct. One needs to be morally upright in one's activities and should not indulge in stealing, murder, sexual misconduct, etc. This is called right action. Action and feeling go hand in hand. Hence, right action is a prerequisite for feeling good and happy.

5. *Right livelihood.* It means that one should not engage in trades or occupations, which result in harm for other living beings. It is about ethical livelihood, which is earned through rightful means. It entails honesty in our business dealings, not try to earn money by cheating, giving bribes, or stealing. We spend most of our lifetime in work; therefore to be ethical is necessary for happiness.

6. *Right effort.* Right effort is necessary to attain anything in life. If we do not give our 100 per cent effort and expect to win in life, it is a road to misery. We need to be persistent on the chosen path and overcome the entire obstacle. Whether you want to succeed in the material world or the spiritual dimension, right effort is the key. Without right effort, one cannot expect to reach the destination.

7. *Right mindfulness.* Right mindfulness is right awareness or right attention. One should be constantly keep themselves alert to events, thoughts, and persons that affect the body and mind. One should be aware of his words, conduct, thinking, behaviour, and action and their repercussions.

8. *Right concentration.* Right concentration. It is also known as right meditation and involves concentration on an object of attention until reaching full concentration and a state of meditative absorption. This results in cutting off the impurities of thoughts and ultimate self-awakening. The right concentration enables a person to go beyond happiness and suffering, likes and dislikes and become a fountain of unconditional love and compassion.

These eightfold path would automatically lead to happiness. Happiness happens when you are truthful to yourself, other and follow the right living, action and thinking. Happiness is a by-product of your action and thought. When you try to achieve directly, you will be tempted towards pleasure. Hence, the focus should be on action rather than result of happiness.

Seven Deadly Sins

Wealth without work
Pleasure without conscience
Science without humanity
Knowledge without character
Politics without principle
Commerce without morality
Worship without sacrifice.

(Mahatma Gandhi)

PART II

Happiness with Self

PRINCIPLE 6

Be Yourself

Many people are living their life not as they want to live. They live their lives according to what others think is best for them; they live their lives according to what their parents, friends, teachers, government, and the media think is best for them. They ignore their inner voice, their calling. The only person who is going to live with you throughout your life is yourself. You are your constant companion. Imagine the pain of disliking that constant companion and trying to become something else to meet the expectations of society and your parents. Look inward—if you truly like yourself, you will be deeply happy and become a fountain of happiness. Always remember *you are unique* in the entire universe.

My Deep Driving Desire

I am what my deep driving desire is.
As my desire is, so is my will.
As my will is, so is my deed.
As my deed is, so is my destiny.

(The Upanishads)

The best and easiest way to know yourself is to know what your deepest desire is. However, the outside pull is so strong that we often succumb to it and lead our entire life on the whims and fancies of society and feel tremendous pressure to toe the line. 'To be yourself in a world that is constantly trying to make you something else is the greatest accomplishment' (Ralph Waldo Emerson).

Be yourself, whatever you are; be firmly established in your unique being. Neither should you be ashamed of yourself nor overly egoistic. Just be truly healed in yourself. That's the key to foundation for long-lasting happiness. Being yourself implies no masking but being transparent. It also implies that you take full responsibility of yourself.

In Shakespeare's *Hamlet*, Polonius says to his son, 'This above all: to thine own self be true. And it must follow, as the night the day, thou canst not then be false to any man.'

When you are driving towards your destination and you hear the voice of your wife saying to take the left and your children to take the right and your parents say halt a bit and go slow, what will happen if you keep listening to them? You will miss the destination. Hence, be guided by your inner voice. Take care of your family members, love them, but know that each of us has a separate destination and mission in life. However, majority of us live life following others and trying to be like them. 'Most people are other people. Their thoughts are someone else's opinions, their lives a mimicry, their passions a quotation' (Oscar Wilde).

'Care about what other people think and you will always be their prisoner'– (Lao Tzu). When you listen too much to other people, you can never follow your inner voice. There is a trade-off between the inner voice and the outer voice. In the end, it is the inner voice that counts for your happiness. To know and follow your calling is very important for lasting happiness. 'The two most important days in your life are the day you are born and the day you find out why' (Mark Twain).

Here's an interesting story from the *Aesop Fables: The Man, the Boy, and the Donkey.*

A man and his son were once going with their donkey to market. As they were walking along by its side, a countryman passed them and said, 'You fools, what is a donkey for but to ride upon?'

So the man put the boy on the donkey, and they went on their way. But soon they passed a group of men, one of whom said, 'See that lazy youngster, he lets his father walk while he rides.'

So the man ordered his boy to get off, and got on himself. But they hadn't gone far when they passed two women, one of whom said to the other, 'Shame on that lazy lout to let his poor little son trudge along.'

Well, the man didn't know what to do, but at last he took his boy up before him on the donkey. By this time they had come to the town, and the passers-by began to jeer and point at them. The man stopped and asked what they were scoffing at. The men said, 'Aren't you ashamed of yourself for overloading that poor donkey with you and your hulking son?'

The man and boy got off and tried to think of what to do. They thought and they thought till at last they cut down a pole, tied the donkey's feet to it, and raised the pole and the donkey to their shoulders. They went along amid the laughter of all who met them till they came to the market bridge, when the donkey, getting one of his feet loose, kicked out and caused the boy to drop his end of the pole. In the struggle, the donkey fell over the bridge, and his forefeet being tied together, he was drowned.

'That will teach you,' said an old man who had followed them. 'Please all, and you will please none.'

When you go with your deepest desire, you strive to be excellent and not superior. The road to excellence is beating your own standards. It is placing you against yourself, challenging your inertia and limited thinking, and flowering your inner true self. 'Try not to become a man of success, but try rather to become a man of value' (Albert Einstein). Flow with your deepest desire, and you will be in harmony with excellence. Go against it and strive for superiority, and you prepare for a miserable life because you cannot be superior all the time, not even in your strength zone. The desire to be superior comes when the motive is to impress others. 'What the superior man seeks is in himself, what the small man seeks is in others' (Confucius).

Here's an interesting story:

Once upon a time, there was a stonecutter who used to make living by breaking stones. He was quite satisfied with his work and simple life.

The nearby mountain had a spirit, which often appeared to men and helped them. The stone-cutter, however, didn't believe and remained uninterested.

One day the stone-cutter carried a gravestone to the house of a rich man and saw the beautiful house and luxuries beyond his imagination. Soon he started feeling his daily work as burdensome, and he said to himself, 'I break these stones, and people use them to build their mansions. I wish that I were a rich man and had a mansion!' And a voice answered him, 'Your wish is heard, a rich man you shall be!' Now he was a rich man and living very happily.

One day, he saw his prince's convoy pass by his mansion. With the grandeur and respect of the prince seated in the royal carriage, he thought, *Oh! If I were only a prince and could go in such a carriage in such a grand way, how happy I should be.*

And the voice of the mountain spirit answered, 'Your wish is heard, a prince you shall be.' As a prince, he began roaming around in his cavalcade. It was now the summer season, so one day he felt very hot inside his carriage. He thought, *The sun is mightier than the prince, oh, if I were only the sun!* The mountain spirit granted his wish; he became the sun. He shot his powerful beams in all directions and enjoyed burning the grass in the fields and discomforting people on earth including prince and kings.

But one day the clouds disguised the sun and obstructed the sun rays reaching the earth. Now he felt the cloud was more powerful than the sun. He wished, 'I would be happy only if I were a cloud.' The mountain spirit granted his wish and he became a cloud. He was very happy to wander as a cloud in the sky and felt mightier than the sun. Soon after, he realized that the strong winds could push away the clouds at their will.

Thus, he thought, *The wind is stronger than the clouds. I would be happy only if I were a wind.* His wish was granted, and he became the wind. He was blowing freely and felt powerful pushing the clouds at will and uprooting trees. But he realized that he could not budge the mountain. The mountain remained standing still and blocked his movement. He felt upset that there was something that was mightier than wind. He wished, 'I would be happy only if I were a mountain.

The mountain spirit fulfilled his wish, and he became a mountain. He felt very powerful as the wind could not affect the mountain. However, after a few days, he saw a stonecutter driving tools into his surface. The stonecutter was hitting at the feet and soon and a great block broke off and fell upon the ground. Now worrying that the man would destroy the mountain bit by bit over time, he realized that the stone cutter was mightier than the mountain. He wished, 'Oh, if I were only a man.' His wish was again granted, and he became a stonecutter again.

He now realized that one must be satisfied with oneself and should not long to be something or somebody else. He learnt that an ambition to be mightier is a never-ending journey that brings dissatisfaction. To make peace with oneself and find happiness in the present moment is far more important.

The grass is always greener on the other side of the fence. The famed actor thinks how wonderful it is to be a minister with a lot of power. The minister thinks how good it is to be an actor, always surrounded by glamorous heroines and people seeking autographs. The rich hanker for power and fame. Hence, when you are not yourself, you venture on a never-ending rat race at the cost of your happiness. The source of all happiness lies in being yourself. When you are yourself, you don't bend over to please others. You recognize that no one is paying as much attention to you as you might think. All are engrossed in their own world with their own problems and fancies. Stop trying to be something that you're not to please others. The moment you accept the real you, you will become authentic and a cynosure. When you are authentic, there will be harmony in your thinking, speech, and actions.

'If you look into your own heart, and you find nothing wrong there, what is there to worry about? What is there to fear?' (Confucius).

PRINCIPLE 7

Do What You Love

'There is only one success—to be able to spend your life in your own way' (Christopher Morley).

We cannot spend our day merely in sleeping, eating, and roaming around aimlessly throughout the day. As humans, we need some constructive work wherein we can involve ourselves. Therefore, work is pivotal for a happy life. But we must do what we love to be happy. Every person must ask himself what his true calling is. What are your true gifts? Operate from your strength, and you will live a happy, meaningful life. 'If you want to live a happy life, tie it to a goal, not to people or objects' (Albert Einstein). The painter Von Gogh, one of the best painters, was under starvation to spend money on paintings. During his lifetime, none of his paintings were sold. However, it didn't matter because he loved paintings, and fame or money were not important to him. He lived in material poverty but experienced the deepest sense of satisfaction because he was doing what he truly loved. Ustaad Bismillah Khan, the famous Shehnai player (a double-reed oboe) and Bharat Ratna, awardee, died in abject poverty but had very fulfilling lives. When you follow your true calling, every work becomes a source of satisfaction, joy, and growth. Work rather defines our very existence. If we don't like what we do, we will end up being miserable and frustrated. All the successful and happy people have followed their mission in life and have lived a fulfilling and vibrant life. 'Choose a job that you like, and you will never have to work a day in your life' (Confucius). Leonardo da Vinci, Beethoven, Mozart, Albert Einstein, Madam Curie, Muhammad Ali, Michael Phelps, and Sachin Tendulkar spent hours in doing what they truly love and created a masterpiece and excellence.

'A man's concern, even his despair, over the worthwhileness of life is an existential distress but by no means a mental disease' (Viktor E. Frankl, *Man's Search for Meaning*). The inner restlessness is satisfied when we do what we deeply love to do and feel immense satisfaction at it. Otherwise, whatever you do, you will not be happy. The precondition of happiness is to be in sync with the song of your soul. If you are not doing what you love and not living life on your terms, it is akin to committing a spiritual suicide. This may look little harsh, but think for yourself. As the profound lines from the Holy Bible say, 'For what shall it profit a man if he shall gain the whole world, and lose his own soul?' Always ask this million-dollar question to gauge whether you are moving in the right track.

'If you follow your bliss, you put yourself on a kind of track that has been there the whole while, waiting for you, and the life you ought to be living is the one you are living' (Joseph Campbell).

Following the inner voice is the surest way to attain lasting happiness. It ensures harmony between your thoughts, actions, and words. A happy person operates from their strength zone and does what he loves. Take life as an organic whole. You cannot fragment life into tight compartments. So if you are engaged in a profession and job that you don't enjoy, you won't feel great about yourself, and sooner or later, the sense of worthlessness will creep in. It would also impact your social and personal life. When you are devoting the major portion of your life into work that you don't enjoy, it is never going to make your life very charming and effective. Whether you accept or not, it is an important pillar of your happiness in life. A person who does what he loves has an altogether different level of energy, enthusiasm, and aura. Most often he would achieve success in doing what he loves with happiness.

PRINCIPLE 8

Freedom—Pull Your Own Strings

In the Hindu religion, it is said that the ultimate aim of life is moksha, i.e. freedom. Pursue your freedom with dogged perseverance. It is one of the fundamental requisites of human beings for real growth and happiness. Freedom is the craving of each soul. It is only in freedom we can bloom to our highest potential. 'Everything that is really great and inspiring is created by the individual who can labour in freedom' (Albert Einstein).

1. *Freedom enhances the sense of well-being. The Happy Planet Index 2012* placed India at 32 whereas China was at 60 despite the fact that China is more economically developed and has a higher longevity. The reason I feel Indian people are happier despite their lower economic position is the freedom they enjoy vis-à-vis the Chinese. The freedom to choose leaders, careers, and marriage partner; express opinions; and free media does augment the sense of well-being. The communist economies are egalitarian and good for masses because they usually have full employment and social security for the senior citizens, yet freedom is so important that the people constantly escape from communist to capitalist countries—from Red China to Hong Kong, from

North Korea to South Korea, from Russia to neighbouring countries.

2. *Inner freedom is the real freedom.* 'No man is free who is not master of himself' (Epicurus). The outward freedom is a reflection of our inner freedom. The outward freedom is in exact proportion to the inward freedom we enjoy or exercise. Meditation is the first and the last freedom because it gives you a hilltop view of your own body and your own mind. It creates a distance between your inner self and the flow of your thoughts. You become a witness of your action, and instead of being engrossed in the action, you become umpire of your own thoughts and actions. Each one craves for freedom and independence. May it be a lover, parent, CEO, or prime minister, the desire for freedom is one of the most fundamental cravings. Desire is an impediment for freedom; desire binds you. If you have many desires, there is no freedom and peace of mind. Ambition is like sand in your eyes or butterflies in your tummy.

3. *Freedom is beyond the feverishness of choice.* In western countries, freedom to choose is being treated at par with freedom. The freedom to choose is further upgraded when you have many choices; 'the more the merrier' is the credo. The freedom to choose food, career, home, travel, and other material comforts and security undoubtedly augments our sense of freedom. But it has its own limitations, since too many choices leads to more confusion and drains our energy. For instance, even if you have 2000 TV channels to choose from, you will be limiting to 5-10 channels most of the time.

The real freedom is freedom from want, the feverishness, which comes out as detachment and contentment.

Freedom is neither unbridled pleasure-hunting nor is it renunciation; both are misnomers. However, they are ubiquitously used as synonyms. The desperate and feverish love to call it pleasure and the depressed ones call it renunciation, a much-misunderstood concept. It is not about denial of good and beautiful things in life. Rather, it is about shedding the feverishness about things and enjoying life as a king rather than a needy beggar. It is about mental clarity and inner peace and progress.

4. *Freedom comes with responsibility and discipline.* Another important factor is that freedom comes with responsibility, though it might seem paradoxical. But it is true that the more responsible you are, the freer you become. But most people do not prefer freedom, as it comes with responsibility. People rather prefer to follow the leaders, social norms, secured jobs only to shirk responsibility. Freedom comes with the boldness of taking responsibility for one's action.

'I am free, no matter what rules surround me. If I find them tolerable, I tolerate them; if I find them too obnoxious, I break them. I am free because I know that I alone am morally responsible for everything I do' (Robert A. Heinlein).

Freedom comes with discipline; without discipline, there can be no freedom. As aptly said, 'Freedom and discipline are opposites and complementary. The purpose of defence is to protect freedom. But is there freedom in defence? Do soldiers have freedom? No, they are totally bound, not even allowed to put the right foot down when told the left foot.

Their steps are measured and they are unable even to walk with a natural rhythm. There is total lack of freedom in defence. That which has absolutely no freedom is protecting the freedom of the country! So it is with the police; they protect the freedom of the individual. But are they free?'

Discipline protects freedom. They both go hand in hand. Understand this and go ahead in life. You have some restrictions, and it is this that allows you freedom. You can choose to focus either on freedom or discipline, and this makes you happy or unhappy. 'Freedom without discipline is like a country without defence . . . Fear of losing freedom also brings defence. The purpose of defence is to eliminate fear' (Sri Sri Ravi Shankar).

Freedom means moving out of prohibition and restriction. However, it is not unfettered action; it is not for the lazy, cowardly, and cautious people. It is for the bold, courageous gamblers of life who can take the chance to move out of their comfort zone.

PRINCIPLE 9

Growth over Safety—Risking

The people in this world can be primarily classified into two different types. One, those who prefer growth over safety, and the other, those who choose safety over growth. The growth-oriented people take the initiative and risk to move to another level of material prosperity and psychological challenges. They are the true leaders. They give up pleasures and strive for lasting joy. They have a higher sense of confidence and achievement. They have tasted the life one-to-one with all its pain and pleasure. Whereas the safety-oriented people run after pleasure; they don't strain too much and are satisfied with their existing condition. They snugly remain in their comfort zone.

Growth is painful because it involves changes and you have to move out of your comfort zone. When a woman gives birth to a child, it is painful. When you prepare for exams, it is painful. When you aspire for Olympic gold, the daily gruelling practice is painful. When you leave home for your own career or marital life, it is painful. But in all the cases, you grow and acquire economic, social, emotional, and spiritual maturity.

'A ship is safe in harbour, but that's not what ships are for' (William G. T. Shedd).

The safety-minded people are like adult elephants that are physically capable of breaking away from chain links tied to posts, but they don't do so. Because since their childhood, they were tied to the same chain links, and when they initially attempted to break the chain, they failed to do so as they were not physically strong. This limitation becomes entrenched, and they get conditioned to accept it as their boundary or limitation. Such self-limiting beliefs are fatal to our growth. You will see millions of people silently suffering the pangs of going for the jobs they don't like. They take it as their destiny simply out of fear of leaving their comfort zone and thereby mortgage their happiness and growth.

'If you always put limits on everything you do, it will spread into your work and into your life. There are no limits. There are only plateaus, and you must not stay there, you must go beyond them' (Bruce Lee, martial artist). If you don't push the limits, the limits would keep on shrinking your space. As someone rightly said, life is the fight for territory.

Whether you like it or not, things around us go on changing, and the risk is inevitable. Playing safe is inimical in the long run. The very notion of safety is illusion. I just love this African saying that says, 'Every day in Africa, a gazelle wakes up. It knows it must run faster than the fastest lion or it will be killed. Every morning a lion wakes up. It knows that it must outrun the slowest gazelle or it will starve to death. It does not matter whether you are a lion or a gazelle. When the sun comes up, you better be running.' Risk is inherent, part and parcel of life. 'Life is either an adventure or nothing' (Helen Keller). Understanding the risks and learning to manage them has been the mantra for survival in any age or in any realm of life. It is one of the most important arts to be learnt to leading a meaningful life. There is no way to avoid it, hence embracing and managing risks is of critical importance and a critical attribute of human beings. All the progress made by human beings in frontiers of science and arts has been by the risk takers.

PRINCIPLE 10

Embrace the Change

Misery arises because we don't allow change to happen. We cling; we want things to be static. If you love a person, you want the person to remain the same way. You want your name, fame, and influence to remain the same. That is how misery arises. Because every moment, change keeps on happening, and nobody can be certain about the next moment.

Holding on to the past is akin to holding a dead dog around your waist. It is not only futile but painful and stupid. Suppose you played with your nephew when he was two years old and you used to fondle and cuddle him, and then you meet him after a decade. Would you still behave with him in the same manner? First, it may not be physically easy to carry him in your arms, and if even you do, he will rebel and hate it, and secondly, neither your nephew nor you would have the same emotional state that both of you had a decade ago.

A wise person knows that life is constantly changing. There is only one thing permanent, and that is change. To accept this nature of life, to accept this changing existence with all its seasons and moods, this constant flow that never stops for a single moment, is the path to happiness. Then nothing can disturb your happiness. Just drop the desire for permanency because it creates unhappiness. The wise accept the change, and in that very acceptance, most of the unhappiness evaporates.

'Viveka is understanding or observation that everything is changing. Whatever I consider stationary or solid, they are changing, nature, every changing reality and a thorough understanding of this is called Viveka . . . Viveka recognizing the changes. Changing nature of surrounding, life in general. This very thing will reduce 99% of the misery' (Sri Sri Ravi Shankar).

'They must often change who would be constant in happiness or wisdom' (Confucius).

Accepting change also means embracing insecurities in life and making the best out of them. There was an inspiring Hindi movie, *Zindagi Na Milegi Dobara* (You Will Not Get Life a Second Time) on how to deal with your deepest fears. It had three characters, and each one had a fear, which they overcame. The movie had a lovely punchline, 'Darr kaey aagey jeet hai,' meaning 'Beyond fears lies victory.' As Ralph Waldo Emerson aptly said, 'Do what you are afraid to do.' Accepting change would also enable you to get rid of past and embrace the present wholeheartedly without fear of the future. With acceptance and courage, one can overcome fear and resistance to change.

PRINCIPLE 11

Live in the Present

An average person lives by hope. He is trained by his parents and society to live that way. A child thinks that he will be happy when he grows up and not bullied by grown-up young kids. When he grows up as a teen, he thinks he will be happy when he will go to college and have many friends and more liberty. When he goes to college and has a girlfriend, he thinks he will be happy when he will have a job and become financially independent. When he gets a job, he thinks he will be happy once he gets married and settled in life. When he gets married, he thinks he will be happy when he will have children. When he has children, he thinks he will be happy once they get settled with good jobs and get married. Now having spent his prime lifetime, he realizes that he has spent all his life in false hope, and he hangs on to the ultimate and final hope: maintaining good health for a peaceful death.

Another type of people spoil their happiness by holding the old grudges and guilt. They hold and nurture these grudges and guilt as if they are precious stones and add to happiness to their life. Their present thinking and action is determined by bad experiences of the past. If they had failed in relationships in the past, they will shut themselves from any intimate relationship. Hence, there are two big enemies of happiness: past and future. 'Things that are done, it is needless to speak about . . . things that are past, it is needless to blame' (Confucius). One of the most important steps towards self-development and eternal happiness is to live in the present. The power of focusing and living in the present moment is gateway to happy and successful life.

'Finish each day and be done with it. You have done what you could. Some blunders and absurdities no doubt crept in; forget them as soon as you can. Tomorrow is a new day. You shall begin it serenely and with too high a spirit to be encumbered with your old nonsense' (Ralph Waldo Emerson).

Sri Sri Ravi Shankar offers a wise way of dealing with past and future: 'Only one who is 100 per cent in doing can recognize the happening. The healthiest way to apply this knowledge is to see the whole past as happening and the present as doing. If you see the past as doing, then ego and regret come along. And when you see the present as happening, then laziness and unawareness set in. If you apply the doing for the future, it brings tension and worry. If you apply the happening for the future, it might bring some confidence and also lethargy. Let the happening be for the past. Let the doing be for the present. And the future is a mix of both.'

The secret of happiness lies in being totally in the present. Be present in everything you do. After all, life is a journey not a destination.

PRINCIPLE 12

Life Is Short

Less is more. The quality of experience is more important rather than the number of years lived. When you are dying, all the things that are irrelevant become useless, and what you have been postponing becomes prominent. The mundane things like sunrise, moon, wife, children, parents, hobbies, etc., assume significance. 'Your time is limited, so don't waste it living someone else's life. Don't be trapped by dogma—which is living with the results of other people's thinking. Don't let the noise of other's opinions drown out your own inner voice. And most important, have the courage to follow your heart and intuition. They somehow already know what you truly want to become. Everything else is secondary' (Steve Jobs).

When you accept the change and inherent insecurity of life, you can enjoy it more fully. The death–ground strategy of Sun Tzu is very useful way of living life in a meaningful way. It says throw your soldiers into positions whence there is no escape, and they will prefer death to flight. If they will face death, there is nothing they may not achieve. Officers and men alike will put forth their uttermost strength. Similarly, when you realize that life is short and insecure, it will bring dynamism to your life. All the unwanted things, distractions, and complaints against others will evaporate. You will not postpone things that bring you greatest happiness. 'Life is either a great adventure or nothing' (Helen Keller). As Sri Sri Ravi Shankar aptly said, 'Spend one day in the cemetery or funeral home. You will have a very close and intense experience of the impermanence of life. Whatever complaints you have will vanish. Having the experience that death can come anytime will change your perspective on life for good.'

Fyodor Dostoyevsky, the greatest author, wrote his best novels after a near-death experience. He and his colleagues were given death sentences for inciting revolution against the czar. However, just before his execution, the news arrived that the death sentence was commuted. He realized the importance of living life to the fullest. He realized the temporariness of life. In India, the Shiva devotee smears bhabhuti (ash) on their forehead every day in the morning after prayer so as to remind them the temporariness of the life.

When I was young, I read a story about an army man who used to live in the borders most of the time. As he was away from his family, he used to feel very sad. He used to always hanker for the company of his family. Every year, he used to visit home two to three times and stay with family for two months. That period used to be the happiest one, whereas while on duty for the rest of the ten months he used to feel miserable. He never enjoyed a single moment of his duty, though he was posted to a picturesque border terrain, and eyed the date of his pension as if it would liberate him of all his misery. Finally, after thirty-five years of his service, the D-Day has come. He got retired from his service, and with high expectations of having a happy time with family, he precede to his home town. However, after a few days, he realized that the scenario had completely changed. The loving wife was no longer a sweet lady but a bickering old lady who loved to fight. The daughters were busy with their married lives and in rearing children. The sons were also focused on their professions and personal lives. The daughter-in-law disliked his presence. Since most of his pension money had been invested in repairing the home, he was left with less money and survived on the meagre pension. He realized that the rosy days of holidays when he used to come with gifts and money did not match the reality after the pension. He then realized the folly of ignoring his days in the service. He never lived in the present for the pipe dream of happiness with family. It was too late for him to recognize that a lot of water had passed under the bridge. He sobbed in silence with tears in his eyes.

This story underlies the importance of realizing the shortness of life, changing dynamics and living in the present rather than mortgaging our happiness to a distant future milestone.

PRINCIPLE 13

Clarity, Brevity, and Totality

One of the bosses of my father was very vengeful and did everything to spoil the career prospects of my father. However, when he came to know that I had been selected for interview for an Indian army officer, the very next day, he called me in his cabin and gave me a nice pompous lecture. However, I still remember his advice and just loved it. He advised me that there were three things that are important to be a good officer or leader: (1) focusing on clarity of the subject, (2) brevity in conversation and writing, and (3) totality of perspective.

Clarity cuts off the distractions or less-rewarding situations, events, and people from our lives. If you have the clarity of your values and priorities in life, you will be less likely to be influenced by the obstacles and distractions. Being decisive is critical for happiness. Indecisiveness saps and creates confusion.

Brevity enables us to express things in a concise manner, and this habit earns us more respect and saves our energy. The eternal principle of 'less is more' is applicable in all spheres of life. The most articulate and most successful people are brief in their speech. The most powerful mantra is the shortest, just two letters of the alphabet, i.e. OM.

The best expression of love is just three words, 'I love you.' The Kumba Mela, which comes after ten years, is the most sought-after spiritual congregation on earth because it is for a few days, and the list goes on and on. 'Good things, when short, are twice as good' (Baltasar Gracián).

The totality of things enables us to embrace contradictions and makes us more generous. 'Wheresoever you go, go with all your heart' (Confucius). Day with night, love with hate, freedom with responsibility, action with inaction, good with evil, sweet with bitter, birth with death, etc. These paradoxical elements make things complete. One is incomplete without the other; rather, they give prominence to each other.

There is an interesting Zen proverb:

> Before enlightenment, I chopped wood and carried water.

> After enlightenment, I chopped wood and carried water.

To understand, we need to know the background story: A man asked a Zen master, 'Since you have become enlightened, what changes happen in your life?' The master said, 'Before I became enlightened, I used to chop wood and carry water from the well.' And the man asked, 'Now that you have become enlightened, what do you do? What changes have happened?' He said, 'I chop wood, and I carry water from the well.' But the man was puzzled. 'Then,' he said, 'what is the difference? It is the same thing.'

And the master laughed. He said, 'It is not the same thing. Before, I used to chop wood and think a hundred and one thoughts. Now when I chop wood, I only chop wood, my mind and thoughts are totally focused. It is so beautiful just to chop wood with totality. Before, I used to have a thousand and one desires while drawing water from the well. Now I simply draw water. And to tell you the truth, there is no one inside me who is drawing the water. And when I am chopping the wood, it is wonderful because there is nobody in me chopping the wood. I have disappeared! The wood is being chopped, and the water is being carried, and it is tremendously beautiful.'

The beauty of life is for those who focus on the moment with totality. The sense of belongingness is just magical. So wherever you go, just belong to the place, people, and nature; you will always be happy.

PRINCIPLE 14

Comfortable with Your Aloneness

The greatest dis-ease of developed society is not physical diseases; it is the emotional starvation of loneliness and resultant hopelessness. The emotional starvation is so acute that senior citizen depends heavily on pets to meet their need of a living company. I felt very sad when I saw a group of old ladies waiting for the metro train in Paris suburbs. Each of them was with their pets wrapped cozily in their arms and baby perambulators as if it were their grandchildren. To love pets is not bad but to depend on pets because your loved ones have deserted you is sub optimal human life. It indicates how much we hanker for the company of others and even ready to substitute it with pets because we cannot handle loneliness.

We are so outward-driven that we just cannot stand to be without people around. Loneliness is the biggest disease. Loneliness and the feeling of being unwanted is the most terrible poverty. Every difficulty is an opportunity. Solitude is immensely healing. When you don't need anybody's attention and are healed in your very self, your individuality becomes charismatic. You are very much happy with your own company; people around would feel that radiance and would be hankering for your presence.

In the western countries where family ties are weakening, the problem of neurosis is on the rise. The neurosis becomes a mechanism to draw attention. The psychiatrists have found a paradox that neurotic people, over a period of time, become dependent on them as their agony aunts and consolers. Consequently, such patients take decades to overcome their neuroses and like to continue to be in somewhat mental doldrums to be able to receive the attention of the psychiatrist. The need for attention is so high among people that they become overdressed, underdressed, wear bright colours, shout, cry, etc. Even murders and robberies are done out of need to prove one's importance besides monetary consideration. Neurosis is a craving for attention. In contrast to psychoanalysts, in Zen monasteries, such neurotics become normal within few weeks. Because in Zen monasteries, no attention is given to the neurotic person; they simply leave him alone. No special attention and importance is given. He is left to himself. Surprisingly, within few weeks, he comes out absolutely normal.

'The ideal man is he who, in the midst of the greatest silence and solitude, finds the intensest activity, and in the midst of the intensest activity finds the silence and solitude of the desert . . . That is the ideal of Karma-Yoga, and if you have attained to that you have really learnt the secret of work' (Swami Vivekananda).

'The word for solitude in Sanskrit is "ekant", meaning "the end of loneliness". Loneliness cannot end by changing company, even if it is more sympathetic and understanding. It can only end when you discover your real nature for yourself' (Sri Sri Ravi Shankar).

There can be another interpretation that in this universe each one is connected to each other. Our fate and happiness is integrated; *alone*, therefore, means 'all-oneness'. You will realize that ocean is in the drop and the ocean is the sum total of all the drops, this feeling of interconnectedness gives utter assurance and happiness. Solitariness then heals instead of threatens. The psychotherapy is layering on layering; it keeps the real issue unaddressed. Rather than curing the problem, giving more attention nurtures the problem. Solitude enables peeling off the attention starvation by simply shifting the focus from outward to inward. When you are alone, the inner voice becomes more vocal. When you hear your own inner voice, it is near impossible to go haywire. The neurotic person moves from being an actor to a witness.

The modern man is so much afraid of being with himself that he loves to remains busy so that he can avoid himself. The 24/7 Internet, mobile phones, newspapers, holidaying, partying, listening to music, etc. are musts to remain engaged. To be alone is just maddening.

Space around me where my soul can breathe
I've got body but my mind can leave
Nothing else matters, I don't care what I miss
Company is okay, solitude is bliss . . .
(song, 'Solitude is Bliss' by Tame Impala)

PRINCIPLE 15

Listening to Body Wisdom

Body is the temple where our divine soul lives. Both are inseparable as they are interlinked. Body is gross mind whereas mind is refined body. However, it is easier to control your body than your mind. 'He that would perfect his work must first sharpen his tools'– (Confucius).

The importance of healthy body for living a happy life cannot be overemphasized. To augment your body wisdom to a peak level, it is important to focus on the following aspects:

Breathing. Breathing is life; it is the door to the universal life force, prana or chi (in Chinese). *Pra* (first unit) *na* (energy) is the vital and primal energy of the universe. The quality of your life is reflected in breathing. It is the most fundamental element of our life. Unfortunately we don't pay any attention to the most important aspect of our life because it is involuntary and requires no effort. As our mental state and feelings are directly reflected in our breathing, we can influence it through our breathing. Deep breathing can immediately calm our mind and deepen the feelings of being grounded with nature. Take control of your breathing and you can control your emotion, attention, and energy. If you are breathing fully, you can live fully and be lively. Whereas if you are breathing shallow, you will be fearful, low on energy, repressive, angrier, and indifferent.

By controlling and improving our breath, we can also increase longevity. Ancient rishis have pointed out that we are born with a number of breaths, and by elongating our breath, we can increase our longevity. For instance, a tortoise's breath is just three times a minute, and it can live for 150 years. Human breath is twenty to thirty times and we live seventy to eighty years, whereas a dog breathes for 150 times and lives ten to twelve years. Breath is an energizing force concerning the matter in our bodies. Breath is our first and foremost energy, carrying over to all the other bodies after reaching the physical body. The mental energy, emotional energy, physical energy, and spiritual energy, all these are types of prana. If one wants to alter any of these structures, one would do so through prana. In Japan, children are taught deep breathing as a method of controlling anger. When you breathe deeply and naturally, you enable the universal energy to flow through you. You become a hollow bamboo, rather a flute, and therefore you will be light and happy, bereft of diseases and sadness.

Be physically active: One of the main reasons for being unhappy and death before our expiry date is sedentary and routine life. The folks of the countryside still look more vibrant and happy, and live longer than the urbanites. The single most important reason is the active physical movement of the countryside people. However, in the cities, the comfortable life surrounded by gadgets has made us couch potatoes, which is taking a heavier toll than we could imagine. Research has unequivocally found that exercise boosts our happiness level, longevity, will power etc. Furthermore, it is absolutely free of cost. The difference between youth and old age is that of movement. Youth loves to move whereas oldies prefer to be sedentary. All the particles in the universe move and even the planets keep revolving around the sun. Movement is the essence of life and being sedentary is associated with death and decay. 'Remember the only sign of life is motion and growth' (Swami Vivekananda). According to Charles Duhigg, author of *The Power of Habit: Why We Do What We Do in Life and Business*, exercise is a keystone habit, which means daily exercise can build foundation for the growth in all other areas of your life. Simply because an active person will be action-oriented and action brings results. Besides, the discipline of exercising daily would spill over to personal and professional life as well.

Positive body language: Can you jump and feel sad at the same time? Can you dance and cry at the same time? Neuro-Linguist Programme (NLP) emphasizes that there are certain body postures linked with each emotion, and if we could change the associated body posture, the corresponding emotion can be generated. Dr Amy Cuddy, researcher at Harvard Business School, in her extensive research has shown how much our body language can make us feel better or worse. She demonstrated through her research that a change in our posture actually changes the levels of cortisol (the stress hormone) and testosterone (the dominance hormone) by a lot. She found that it only takes two minutes of holding either a high-power pose or a low-power pose to change those levels dramatically.

Whenever you observe incongruence between words and body language of a person, believe the body language, since we are not yet able to mask our body language as we do our words.

Sleep more. The biggest causality of modern life is sleep deprivation. The invention of electricity, Internet, the mobile phone, and television has taken heavy toll on human sleep. Today very few people follow the recommended eight or more hours of sleep each night. The consequences of this chronic lack of sleep are deleterious. The Chinese, Russians, and Germans have used sleep deprivation for torture, which is among the worst of its kind. Lack of sleep drains a person physically and mentally. Adequate sleep augments the sense of well-being, strengthens the immune system, and improves memory and concentration. Good sleep prevents heart attacks and diabetes. Most of the road accidents are due to inadequate sleep. The emergence of IT industry and call centres has led to sleep deprivation among the youth, and it was observed that night shifts and lack of adequate sleep resulted in early aging, high stress, and being burnt out at the age of 40. I personally experienced the pang of sleep deprivation when I had to work on the night shift for one and half month. I can vouch for the tremendous negative effect it has on our health, mind, and sense of well-being. Hence, sleep extra and do away with your accumulated sleep arrears, and it is again a free luxury.

Here's a powerful hand mudra (hand gesture), which is very effective for increasing the physical vitality:

1. Pran Mudra

The Pran Mudra generally increases vitality, reduces fatigue and nervousness, and improves vision. On the mental-emotional level, it increases assertiveness and healthy self-confidence, and gives us courage to start something new and the strength to see things through.

PRINCIPLE 16

Meditation

One of the finest things that have happened to me was the practice of meditation. As they say, in suffering lie the keys to growth. One of my relatives was undergoing severe depression for two years during 2002–2004. It was during his desperate experiments ranging from heavy exercises, skipping food, watching late-night movies, reading spiritual books, medicines, etc., that finally, he gave a shot to meditation. I owe most of my learning to him.

Since he was struggling with lot of stress, he started practicing meditation and recommended the same to me. However, I was sceptical and used to argue back that everything is good if it is done as per the age. Youth is not for meditation. After our sixties anyway, we will find ourselves more inclined to meditation and spirituality. I used to quote the Indian Varna System wherein the ages up to one hundred years is divided into four parts: twenty-five years for learning, twenty-five to fifty years for family life, fifty to seventy-five years for preparation to move towards isolation, and seventy-five to one hundred years for Sannayis.

However, after much discussion, I also decided to give it a try. Believe me, within a few weeks, I was altogether a different person. Something very subtle had shifted deeper.

One day I was travelling in a police truck, as my father was in the police. I was not looking at the passing buildings, people, or shops; rather, I was witnessing them. It was a great realization about the impact of meditation. Furthermore, I become more convinced and started practising it regularly and started experiencing more changes in me. On several occasion, while I was practicing meditation on the terrace, I felt totally weightless. I had awareness of only my crossed palms and feet while sitting in Padmasana. I felt as light as few grams. It was among the best decision. Since then, I have practised meditation regularly. Over a period of time, the level of stress and jitteriness had dwindled, and my stomach problem also started to vanish. Meditation nourishes each cell of your body and strengthens the mind. 'I admit that thoughts influence the body' (Albert Einstein).

Meditation is the easiest, surest, and cheapest way to happiness. As I said, all the wonderful things in world are free, absolutely free. Nature does not discriminate. The body is gross and easier to control. You cannot be happy in an unhealthy body. We are neither just mind nor just body but a combination of both. Both reinforce each other. For total harmony and happiness, both should be in a healthy state. The inherent contradiction: the body is more static, and the mind is more erratic. The body loves routine, whereas the mind loves variety. It is meditation that brings the total harmony between the body and the mind.

PART III

Happiness with Others

PRINCIPLE 17

Relationships—Essence of Human Life

Life is about relationships. The quality of our relationships determines the quality of our life. However, the fountain of all relationships is dependent on the state of your relationship with yourself. That is the fundamental difference between the approach of western world and the eastern world. The former has emphasized looking outward or the other for relationship, whereas the latter has primarily focused inward or the self.

'Relationships are all there is. Everything in the universe only exists because it is in relationship to everything else. Nothing exists in isolation. We have to stop pretending we are individuals that can go it alone' (Margaret Wheatley).

Be fulfilled with yourself, and then go on spill over the love, attention, and resources. You will be always happy and feel the kinglike grandeur. The golden rule is 'to handle yourself, use your head, to handle others, use your heart' (Eleanor Roosevelt). Know that there are two aspects of a person, the sky aspect and the cloud aspect. The sky represents our innermost being, which is pure and loving, whereas the cloud represents the outer action and emotion, which is always in the flux of change. Focus on the sky of a person and not the momentary clouds of his behaviour and words. When you know that everybody is fighting a tough battle, you will have compassion. Never judge a person from the first meeting or his appearance and behaviour. Focus on the better aspect of a person. 'If you judge people you have no time to love them' (Mother Teresa). People are more than their behaviours.

'In true intimacy you stop looking at the act and you start being in love. So if you have determined to love somebody, do not even think whether they love you or not. You love them. That is enough. If they kick you to see whether the love in you is true or not, then you should have more happiness. Then, also, you give love back' (Sri Sri Ravi Shankar).

As African proverb says, 'It's not what you call me, but what I answer to.' Good behaviour is not an investment in the future; rather, it gives immediate happiness. Many people ask, I always behave nicely, but people around don't. They ask people to take good behaviour as a sign of weakness and respond with rudeness, so what is the benefit of good behaviour? The good behaviour brings instant reward in the form of happiness and a peaceful mind, whereas the people who behave badly never enjoy peace of mind. One cannot feel good by behaving bad. They are restless and fickle. That is their punishment or the cost they pay for their bad behaviour.

Love means the art of being with others. Your ability to get along with people greatly impacts the quality of your life in terms of happiness and success. The ability to get along with all types of people is true gift. It requires lots of wisdom and tact to manoeuvre through the human landscape. The test is not to get along with good people but rather all types of people. Know these fundamental truths that everyone is out there furthering their own agenda and goal. If you want the other person to do things for you or behave as per your convenience, you must deliver some benefits. Benjamin Franklin learned his way to swim through the social jungle by adopting empathy towards others rather than his innate charm. Thinking from others' perspective gives you a wide glimpse of his ego, desires, frustrations, and fears shaping his personality. Instead of thinking why it happened to me, you will start thinking why he behaved in certain manner and be able to predict his action and nature more accurately. Accept the people you don't like. Everybody has its own justification and realities; just accept them instead of allowing them to irritate you and diminish your happiness.

Walt Whitman, an American poet, essayist, and journalist, was told again and again that 'your statements are contradictory'.

In response, he said, 'Yes, I am contradictory because I am vast enough to contain contradictions. You are little, you cannot contain contradictions—that's why you are so much troubled. I am not troubled—I am vast enough, contradictions can coexist in me.' Accept life as it is in its totality. If you side with positive aspect of life, the negative aspect would control you. Just like a hungry man always thinks about the food. Embrace the totality: life and death, love and hate, happiness and unhappiness, agony and ecstasy. Paradoxically, if you are too averse towards negative things, it will result in thinking too much about negative things. Human relationships are all about selfishness and politics; embrace them fully.

'Do not let politics sway you away from the path. If you are afraid of politics you cannot be successful in the spiritual realm. You have to cross the barricade of politics. It is a test of your strength, your commitment and your focus . . . When you recognize politics in any group, it is a blessing for you to be centred and to go inward. You can do that without blaming the group, without running away from people, without giving up. It can enhance your skill to act and to remain detached . . . It enhances your capacity to accept and tolerate. It makes you realize that all of life is a game . . . The strong will smile through the politics and the weak will lament' (Sri Sri Ravi Shankar).

One of the easiest ways of experiencing happiness is to give and contribute to others' life and progress. As I said, there is no other; all are one. When you give happiness, there are three ways you receive happiness. First, while giving, the focus gets shifted from you to them, and you tend to forget your misery, unhappiness, and regrets for the moment. Second, when the other person becomes happy, it touches you as well, and finally, when he reciprocates your help immediately or later in the future, you again feel better. Further, it creates a channel of happiness in the future because now you know that you have a good connection with that person.

'If you want happiness for an hour, take a nap. If you want happiness for a day, go fishing. If you want happiness for a month, get married. If you want happiness for a year, inherit a fortune. If you want happiness for a lifetime, help someone else'– (Chinese proverb).

'To get the full value of joy, you must have someone to divide it with' (Mark Twain).

There are two kinds of love. C. S. Lewis has divided love into these two kinds: need-love and gift-love. The need-love depends on the other; you use the other as a means for your nourishment. The gift-love has emphasis on how to give more. Giving brings out the best in your inner being.

Giving enriches both the giver and the receiver. It generates the positive feeling of gratitude, and it is reciprocated. One of the best examples of reciprocation of obligations was the story of five thousand dollars of relief aid that was exchanged between Mexico and Ethiopia. In 1985, Ethiopia faced the worst crisis where thousands were dying from disease and starvation. However, despite the ruination in Ethiopia, the Ethiopian Red Cross had sent the money to help the victims of that year's earthquakes in Mexico City (1985) because in 1935, Mexico had sent aid to Ethiopia when it was invaded by Italy.

Live with abundance mentality and not with scarcity mentality. Abundance does not imply material resources or richness. It simply means resourcefulness like positive attitude, loving nature, courage, and confidence. People crave for genuine love and cooperation rather than expensive gifts. Paradoxically, people would despise your attempt to compensate for your lack of feelings with a beautifully wrapped gift. The innermost craving is about attention, love, and care, and you can do so even without much money in your pocket. Viktor Frankl has illustrated an instance of human abundance that can be practised even in the most brutal concentration camp. He said during his days in the camp, they were given soup with few peas, and many times, some of them did not get any peas. In that utter scarcity of food, every bit of food is critical for your existence as they were sorted daily and the weaker would be sent to the death chamber. Despite this, there were a few who would share their peas with the weaker fellow being. Now that's the abundance mentality. Further he described that inner freedom is about what we choose each moment. He observed that even while going for the death chamber, some entered with a prayer and a smile on their face while others went with fear and curses. So essentially, it is we who carry our weather with ourselves rather than the weather deciding our mood.

In relationships, remember that company does matter and it makes a huge impact on your happiness. This is the easiest way to uplift your immediate and long-term happiness level. Moving around with good people will enrich your life and raise the motivation and morale.

Who you are is reflected by the type of company you keep. 'Birds of a feather flock together.' If you like being happy, you will not surround yourself with sad people. The mismatch of wavelengths would either force you to leave such people or succumb to their habits of being sad and cynical about everything. 'You are the average of the five people you spend the most time with' (Jim Rohn). The arithmetic is simple; if you surround yourself with happy people, you will be happy. Now you know the benefit of being with happy and wise people. You must also know the cost of being with the sad and depressed people. We can call them evil persons from the happiness perspective because they are like coal—when they are hot (angry), they burn (harm) you, and when they are cold (passive), they blacken (bring bad repute to) your hands. Such company always demeans and harms you directly or indirectly. They drain you along with your energy and intellect. The best way to deal with such people is to quietly avoid and ignore them. They are worth neither your love nor hate.

The simple story of the eagle and the chicken illustrates the message:

A fable is told about an eagle who thought he was a chicken. When the eagle was very small, he fell from his nest. A chicken farmer found the eagle, brought him to the farm, and raised him with chickens. The eagle grew up imitating the chickens, believing he was one. One day, the eagle chick looked up at the sky. He saw an eagle flying majestically and effortlessly with its powerful wings. He enquired about the bird. The chicken said, 'That's the king of the birds, the eagle. We're only chickens.' The eagle chick lived and died a chicken because he believed itself to be a chicken due to the company of chickens.

The people you hang out with will either pull you up or pull you down. If you hang out with people who are depressed and frustrated, chances are you will also start up being cynical about life. 'Never argue with an idiot. They will only bring you down to their level and beat you with experience' (George Carlin). Choose your engagement with people wisely. Wise people apply their wisdom. Before any action, they always ponder: Is it worth doing? What would be the repercussion and cost benefit analysis in terms of emotion, finance, relation, and time? Don't focus on small Stuff. Never let your ego determine your action; otherwise, you will lose many battles. The history is full of examples where the mighty nations like the USA fought the useless battles like that of Vietnam, Iraq, and Afghanistan and incurred a huge loss of money and resources. Ed Tate, the world champion of public speaking in 2000, has an interesting way of dealing with and avoiding the negative people. Whenever he sees a negative person around, he pulls his snap-wrist rubber band to trigger the alertness towards the negative aura of such person.

The company of good people is extremely critical for your happiness and progress in life. The importance of being around wise people cannot be overemphasized; it is well captured by this line: 'A single conversation with a wise man is better than ten years of study' (Chinese proverb). Hence, it is important to choose wisely the company you spend your time with. They would also help to bounce back from low morale and bad times. You can learn the value of sacrifice, perseverance, and commitment coupled with love, compassion, and forgiveness. Thus you will know how to succeed and be happy in life. However, it is not possible to interact only with good people; you come across several people, both good and bad, and the sheer number can sap your vital energy. For instance, travelling in crowded trains and buses or having to shop in the crowded places, etc., is very draining. So maximise your interaction with good people and accept the existence of bad people without giving them too much attention.

PRINCIPLE 18

Compassion, despite Knowing Human Nature

The root of unconditional love is compassion. It is the ultimate flowering of human love. In love there is expectation because the dynamic involves give and take. Whereas in compassion, it is only giving, and there is no expectation of receiving. You feel grateful towards the receiver because he has enabled you to offload your overflowing love. When you develop compassion, you are like a flower that unconditionally spreads its fragrance. You don't distinguish. The most important thing to remember is that compassion is not charity or a feel-good factor. It is the finest expression of being. Its consideration is not whether to do good to others or not. The consideration of compassionate people is that you have so much of love, which should only be shared lest it will be wasted and diminish.

Compassion enables you to see that 'behind every culprit, there is a victim crying for help. You need to identify the victim and heal him' (Sri Sri Ravi Shankar). When you are compassionate, you will able to hear the cry of every human's heart saying, 'Love me most when I deserve it least—that is when I need it most' (Swedish proverb). It is just like a stock analyst or the fund manager who makes the most of buying when the stock falls because when that stock revives, it gives him manifold returns. Similarly, when you invest in people during their bad times, they will remember you throughout their lives.

'If you want one year of prosperity, grow grain. If you want ten years of prosperity, grow trees. If you want one hundred years of prosperity, grow people' (Chinese proverb).

We know by our experience that people around us are unreasonable and self-interest. They become friendly when you are successful and wealthy and they turn away when you become poor and fail. Honesty and transparency tend to make you vulnerable in your personal as well as professional life. People are humble while borrowing money and turns indifferent and arrogant when you ask them to return money. People around despise your fame, wealth and success. All these are facts. But despite that love them, help them. Because in doing so you are developing yourself as a good person and your goodness would be reciprocated sooner or later.

When we feel love and kindness toward others, it not only makes others feel loved and cared for, but it helps us also to experience inner happiness and peace. We often use a double standard for ourselves and for others, which creates heartache and unnecessary competition. Compassion enables you to think from the other person's perspective. The Buddhist practice of metta, meaning loving kindness, is very effective in creating a happy life. Metta is indeed a universal, unselfish, and all-embracing love.

Patience with a let-go attitude and thinking from others' point of view develops compassion. Besides, meditation is the fastest way to become more compassionate.

Patience is power.
Patience is not an absence of action;
rather it is 'timing'
it waits on the right time to act,
for the right principles
and in the right way.
(Fulton J. Sheen)

It is easier to talk about love and compassion when all the people around are good and reciprocate our gesture. We humans are driven by self-interest. We think it appropriate and okay when it comes to our decisions and interest. However, when the same principle is followed by others, we feel disappointed. 'A fly before his own eye is bigger than an elephant in the next field' (Chinese proverb). Further, in our social interaction with people we look for the maximum gain at the minimum cost. That's why the rich, powerful, and famous people have a greater following, and the weak and poor are sidelined. We are more courteous while taking debt but become more casual when it comes to paying back. People forget our good deeds quicker and remember our wrong deed longer. We are all salespersons pitching for our interest all the time. We are power-mongers and love to pull the strings. To be precise, we are not fair, and every one of us, therefore, feels life is unfair. It is the fundamental truth of life.

The unfairness of life is to be accepted and not denied or despised. The denial of unfairness of life is like living in the well-lit house and denying the darkness of night outside. It is a childish way of living in airy-fairy utopia. Despising unfairness would only attract more unfair incident in your life. You get what you love or hate because in both the cases you are giving your emotional energy out to the things and the same comes back to your life. Further, when you hate unfairness of life, you would become more unreasonable and therefore people around you would seem more unfair. The best approach is to accept the existence of unfairness in life and take it as challenge or test of your goodness. Keep on doing good and you will transcend the unfair people, events and circumstances in life.

The next step is to accept life as it is without complaining and deal with intelligence. The following story beautifully illustrates on how to deal with the world:

The Snake and a Holy Man

There was a village where one snake used to live. This snake used to keep biting people, and all villagers were very scared of him. So the people of the village never used to venture out of the house much because of the snake; even children used not to play outside their houses.

One day, one holy man was passing through the village, and he was surprised to see the village so quiet, and upon enquiring, he got to know about the snake. So this holy man went to talk to the snake. He explained to him that it was not a good idea to be biting people around and harassing other living beings. It was against the scriptures and he might suffer in his next birth. The snake was very impressed with the holy man, and he promised that he was going to change himself and become a really good snake.

One year ahead . . .

The holy man was again passing through the same village, and he saw the village full of activity. As he went forward, he saw a group of children crowded around the same snake, and they were hitting him with stones and catching its tail, and the snake looked completely tortured.

The holy man drove all the kids away and felt very sorry for the snake. He asked the snake what happened. The snake said that as people started realizing that the snake had stopped biting, they started making fun of him and harassing him.

Then the holy man told the snake, 'I had only asked you to stop biting but not to stop hissing, you have to be nice but still stand your ground.'

Moral of the story: Be nice to people, but don't get walked over.

PRINCIPLE 19

The Power of Words Self-Talk and Conversation with Others

In one of the African countries, the tribal society curses at the tree when they want wood. The tree automatically dies and decays, and then the tribal society picks the wood. Give up your self-defeating self-talk. The negative words sap your morale and inject lots of pain, sadness, and depression in your subconscious mind. More than any disease, it is the negative self-talk that is hurting us most.

'The heart of a fool is in his mouth, but the mouth of a wise man is in his heart'—(Benjamin Franklin).

Research has shown that the Maha Mrityunjaya mantra improves health and increases happiness and peace of mind. It awakens a healing force and removes obstacles. Dr Masaru Emoto, in his well-researched book, *The Miracle of Water*, gives thoughtful insights on the power of words on water. He demonstrated that when water is exposed to good words, good crystals result. He further mentioned that words are vibrations, and when our bodies, comprising of 70 per cent water, are exposed to good words, we experience health and well-being. On the same line, negative words create bad vibrations. Hence, the choice of words creates the corresponding life. Masaru Emoto demonstrated that the most beautiful crystals are those formed after the water is exposed to the words *love* and *gratitude*.

Here's an example, if people around you keep on saying that you are a bad person, after some time, it will settle in your subconscious mind, and soon you will start believing and behaving in the same manner, popularly called the Pygmalion effect or Rosenthal effect. It is the phenomenon of self-fulfilling prophecy whereby the greater the expectation placed upon people, the better they perform. A corollary of the Pygmalion effect is the golem effect, in which low expectations lead to a decrease in performance.

Robert Rosenthal and Lenore Jacobson's study showed that if teachers were led to expect enhanced performance from children, then the children's performance was enhanced. This study supported the hypothesis that reality can be positively or negatively influenced by the expectations of others, called the observer-expectancy effect. Rosenthal argued that biased expectancies could affect reality and create self-fulfilling prophecies.

'If you the change the way look at things, the things you look at change' (Wayne Dyer). The best way to deal with people is to maintain silence when you are angry and to express appreciation in instances of good action. The power of words is immense; if you keep on saying good things about people around, they will behave in the same manner. You can use words wisely and create a desired reality for you and make people support that reality.

PRINCIPLE 20

Detachment—Letting Go and Acceptance

Attachment and expectation is one of the biggest causes of unhappiness. When we are too attached, we overlook the truth that we don't own others. Howsoever close the person may be, i.e. children, spouse, friends, or others, don't feel that they are obliged to reciprocate your love and toe the line because you have done so much for them. Treat them with gratitude that they have shared love with you. Detachment works as a shock absorber. There can be no suffering once this distance is established between you and others and outside events. Be a witness to all your thoughts and the good and bad events. Detachment is not indifference but it is, rather, absence of feverishness, the tendency to control and use the other person for your comfort. It is loving another person without the expectation of return. The focus on detachment is on giving without controlling. Detachment begets centeredness. It is interesting to know that *health* in Sanskrit is *swastha*; that means 'one who is established in oneself'. *Swa* means 'self'; *stha* means 'one who is established in self'. This state is called *swasthya*: total health, which is not just confined to the body but also entails a peaceful and steady state of mind. When you are centred, you will observe that everything around you is changing, and with detachment comes acceptance of change. True freedom is the inner freedom, which can be attained when you are fully aware about your inner world and detached from the worldly events. That does not mean that you have to leave the worldly experience and happiness but be in the world without being affected by it. Be like a lotus, which grows in the mud but is distinct from the mud. 'Little things affect little minds' (Benjamin Disraeli).

Besides accepting change, detachment enables us to let go of being right and the need for control, as most of us spend lot of mental energy in proving others that they are right and want to control them. However, it is impossible for any person to have his way all the time with all the people, and when we don't succeed, we feel either angry or sad. The attempt to be always right and controlling events, people, and circumstances is a chimera. Therefore, such a tendency saps lot of energy and mental peace. Remember, being free is more important than being right. When you give up the need to always be right and control everything that happens to you, you give up on blame: Stop living in illusion, and stop giving your powers away. Just start taking responsibility for your life and life as it is. 'By letting it go, it all gets done. The world is won by those who let it go. But when you try and try. The world is beyond winning' (Lao Tzu).

When we are not consistent with our thoughts, mood, and action, how can we expect other people to behave, think, and feel the way we do? It is impossible and a door to perennial sadness and frustration. The more you have the tendency to control people, events, and circumstances around, the more miserable you will be. First, people will resist and desist too much of interference and, instead of toeing the line, would rebel. Second, the events happen on the macro level due to various causes that are beyond your control. Third, circumstances cannot be created as per our desires simply because of two aforesaid reasons that people behave as per their self-interest and events happen due to multifarious reasons. To change other people is one of the most tiresome exercises. On the contrary, if you become more accepting towards them, they will change. Everything is undergoing changes moment by moment. We cannot control the outside events, circumstances, and people. What is in our control is to manage our reaction and attitude. Letting go is one the most beautiful things for a peaceful and happy life. It brings happiness to you as well as people whom you accept unconditionally. 'God grant me the serenity to accept the things I cannot change, courage to change the things I can, and wisdom to know the difference' (Reinhold Niebuhr).

'Life has no other discipline to impose, if we would but realize it, than to accept life unquestioningly. Everything we shut our eyes to, everything we run away from, everything we deny, denigrate or despise, serves to defeat us in the end. What seems nasty, painful, evil can become a source of beauty, joy and strength, if faced with an open mind. Every moment is a golden one for him who has the vision to recognize it as such' (Henry Miller).

Letting go of false beliefs and ego is important for attaining true happiness. When you hold on to false beliefs and ego, you get stuck in it and you refuse to see the reality. Accepting your false perception and approach towards life and people and letting open up the possibility of moving away from falsehood to reality brings happiness.

PRINCIPLE 21

Respect the Power of Negative and Protect Your Peace of Mind

The negative is always more powerful, at least in the short term. The destruction is always easier and faster than construction. Furthermore, we are conditioned to see mistakes in personal and professional life. The sadness is sapping; it's a major dragger, and it takes a multifold dose of positive action and feelings to maintain the level of happiness. The sadness comes with a heavy cost. Sadness is much more powerful than happiness. One sad moment saps all the happiness of the moment, and it requires many happy moments to overcome the hangover of sadness. As Viktor Franklin in his book *Man's Search for Meaning*, he has observed that 'to draw an analogy, a man's suffering is similar to the behaviour of a gas. If a certain quantity of gas is pumped into an empty chamber, it will fill the chamber completely and evenly, no matter how big the chamber. Thus suffering completely fills the human soul and conscious mind, no matter whether the suffering is great or little. Therefore the "size" of human suffering is absolutely relative.' Sadness is akin to one black dot on your white shirt, and it is enough to take away the focus if you are not alert towards the inherent negative bias. We tend to give more attention to negative things. Negativity overpowers our intelligence and the positive experiences. Therefore, the goal of happiness needs effort on both fronts, increasing the happiness and reducing the sadness.

No argument is worth losing your peace of mind. In any conversation, determine the end result, the gains and losses. If you know that advising your colleagues, family members, is not going to have any impact, don't waste your energy. Brian Tracy uses the term ROE, i.e. return on energy. Is it worth your attention, speech, and action? Let ROE be your yardstick. 'I will not let anyone walk through my mind with their dirty feet' (Mahatma Gandhi). Usually we say, 'Don't hate anybody!' Do you know why you shouldn't hate someone? When you hate someone, their impression becomes strong in you. You become like them. 'Not hating someone is not for their sake. Your hatred makes you become like them' (Sri Sri Ravi Shankar). Always ring fence yourself from negative people, events, and circumstances, and it will save your essential energy, your time and effort.

Thousands of *no* for one *yes* to your happiness: Life is a gift, and you have to treasure it. Engage your life in realizing your full potential and doing what you love. That is one of the major pillars of happy life. If you want to say yes to your fulfilling dream life then you have to protect it by thousands of no to other people demands and distractions. Basically, it means taking charge of your life and setting yourself and your priorities straightforward and setting required boundaries for the same.

'Lock your door rather than suspect your neighbour' (Lebanese proverb).

As Robert Schullar has correctly said, 'Never give leadership role to others, take command and lead from the front.' There will be thousands of demands on your time and energy by the family members, friends, and office colleagues and initially saying no may seem wrong, bad, or guilt-inducing. However, these are the tacit persuasion and pressure techniques used by others to meet their demands and interests. I am not suggesting that don't help, but do it as per your convenience and available time. You have to take care of priorities before taking care of others. 'Things that matter most must never be at the mercy of things that matter least' (Johann Wolfgang von Goethe). Don't surrender your role of navigating your life to outside forces. Lead yourself first, and be the leader for your progress and dreams.

When you are not laser-focused on their mission and goal of happy and fulfilling life, you become available for more demands of other people. You will end up wasting your precious time in trivia and cater to the demands of others. As Anthony Robbins said, it is not that people demand more from you because you are willing but because you are more accessible for more demands. So engage in attaining your full potential instead of fulfilling the demands and wishes of others.

Being selfish is a prerequisite for your growth in the initial phase when you are building yourself up. 'What people say is irrelevant. Who you are is relevant. Never compromise with your inner delight, because that is going to decide who you are. Always go in and look at what you doing to yourself' (Osho). Hence, be a warrior to protect your peace of mind. Be on the alert on the negative and energy-sapping people and events and fight for your inner treasure of happiness.

We can draw profound message from Rabindranath Tagore's Juta Abishkar or the poem 'Shoe Invention'. The message is given below.

Once upon a time, there was a king who ruled a prosperous country. One day, he went for a trip to some distant areas of his country. When he was back to his palace, he complained that his feet were very painful because it was the first time that he went for such a long trip, and the road that he went through was very rough and stony. He then ordered his people to cover every road of the entire country with leather. Definitely, this would need thousands of cows' skin, and it would cost a huge amount of money. Then one of his wise servants dared himself to tell the king, 'Why do you have to spend that unnecessary amount of money? Why don't you just cut a little piece of leather to cover your feet?' The king was surprised, but he later agreed to his suggestion, to make a 'shoe' for himself. There is actually a valuable lesson of life in this story: to make this world a happy place to live, you'd better change yourself—your heart and not the world.

It is better to shield your inner peace rather than fight with the negative events and people and trying to correct them. Shun the world war and protect your happiness at all costs.

Happiness Is Free

Do meditation.
Attend free yoga classes.
Run and participate in a marathon or run anywhere for free.
Go trekking or to any wild destination.
Follow your hobbies.
Smile more.
Speak well about others.
Help others.
Take struggles as challenges.
Avoid unpleasant people and events.
Live in the present.
Accept change and let go.
Sleep well.

Above all,

be joyous in aloneness, ekant, the end of loneliness. Love your company, and it will open the infinite source of happiness, which will be self-manufactured and not imported from others.

I have my kept my promise in describing how happiness is free and easy to attain; now it's up to you to resolve to seek happiness and attain it freely and easily.

Feedback and comments can be sent to
provinkami@yahoo.com